Designed by Mark Wasserman and Irene Ng of Plinko.

Manufactured in Singapore.

10 9 8 7 6 5 4 3 2 1

Library of Congress Cataloging-in-Publication Data is available.

Published by the HOW Series, Dedicated to the Exploration and Dissemination of Unbelievable Brilliance.

Photographs of Dr. and Mr. Haggis-On-Whey by Meiko Arquillos.
Cover illustration by Michael Kupperman.

Thank you to all the men and women who gave us UPN's Eve. **Directors**: Mary Lou Belli; Leonard R. Garner v. (as Lenny Garner); Micheline Lanctôt; Ted Lange; Jody Margolin; Arlene Sanford; Lee Shallat Chemel; Ken Whittingham; Angela Barnes Gomes; Brian K. Roberts. **Writers**: Michael Ajakwe Jr.; Tiffany Anderson; Trish Baker; Randi Barnes; Adrienne Carter; Meg DeLoatch; Judy Dent; David W. Duclon; Anthony C. Hill; Janis Hirsch; Torian Hughes; Walt Kubiak; Clay Lapari; Vivien Mejia; Gary Menteer; David Podemski; Katina Weaver. **Cast**: Eve; Shelly Williams; Jason Winston George (as Jason George); Ali Landry; Natalie Desselle; Brian Hooks; Sean Maguire. **Produced by**: Trish Baker; Troy Carter; Meg DeLoatch; David W. Duclon; Eve; Bob Greenblatt (as Robert Greenblatt); Anthony C. Hill (season 3); Janis Hirsch; Torian Hughes; David Janollari; James Tripp-Haith; Ioanna Vassiliadi. **Original Music**: Missy 'Misdemeanor' Elliott; Jae Staxx; Armique S. Wyche. **Cinematography**: Gary D. Scott. **Film Editing**: Jim McQueen. **Casting**: Mary V. Buck (2004); Wendi Matthews (2004-5); Elizabeth Melcher (as Liz Melcher); Nelia Morago; Holly Powell. **Art Direction**: Jerry Dunn. **Set Decoration**: Bill Mitchell, Chris Sylos. **Costume Design**: Zina Moore-McGlockton, Kara Saun, Tracey White (2005-2006); **Makeup Department**: Veronica Lorenz (makeup assistant department head), Rea Ann Silva (makeup artist), Sean Smith (hair stylist). **Production Management**: Barry F. Boyd; Brian Whitley. **Second Unit Director or Assistant Director**: Terrille Bazile (as Terrill Bazile). **Art Department**: William W. King (as William King); Ronnie Lombard, property master; **Other crew**: Christine Bean, George M. Chappell, Chad Darnell, Danielle De Jesus, Ryan Dean, Ellen Deutsch, Missy 'Misdemeanor' Elliott, Robin Finn (as Robin Anthony), Helen Geier (as Helen Diament), Sandy Gomes, Kellie Griffin.

www.haggis-on-whey.com
www.mcsweeneys.net

ISBN-10 1-932416-39-0
ISBN-13 978-1-932416-39-8

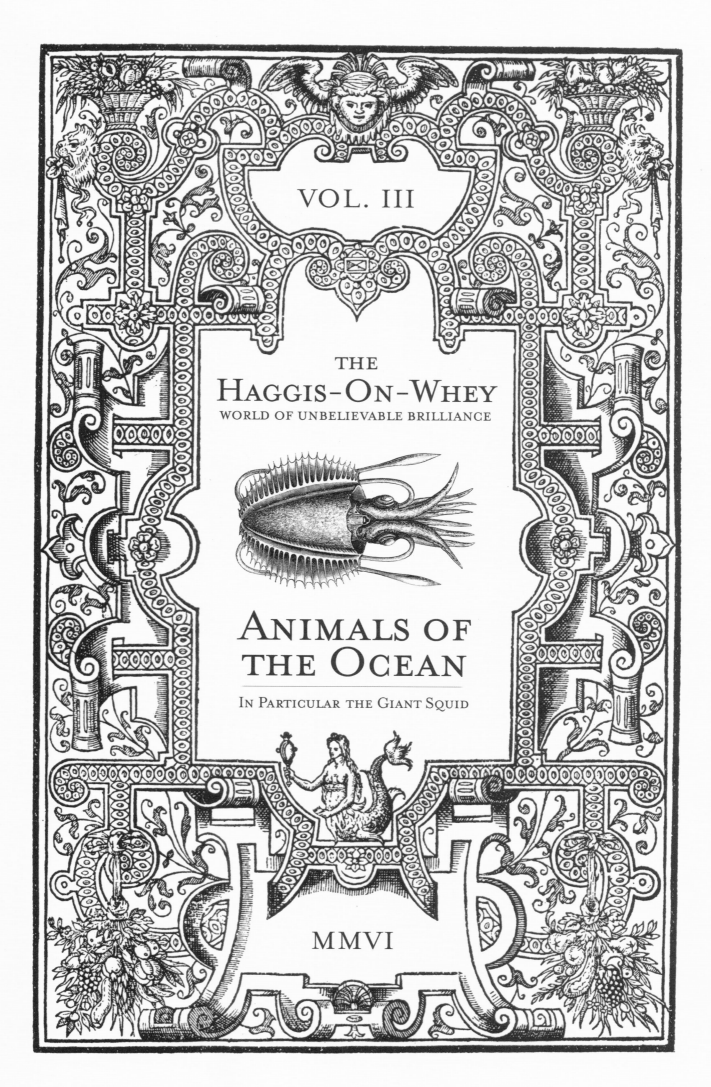

VOL. III

THE
HAGGIS-ON-WHEY
WORLD OF UNBELIEVABLE BRILLIANCE

ANIMALS OF THE OCEAN

In Particular the Giant Squid

MMVI

WELCOME! TO
DR. AND MR. DORIS HAGGIS-ON-WHEY'S
WORLD OF UNBELIEVABLE BRILLIANCE

Dear Reader,

You have purchased this book and now you will learn. My name is Dr. Haggis-on-Whey and I am a scientist; I will not pretend to be your friend. We are here to study animals of the ocean and I will not mince words. If you pay attention I will be less dissatisfied.

The ocean has been on the earth for thousands of years. It is generally blue and nearly always viscous. Most people feel that the ocean is not interesting to study because of these factors, but I think the ocean is not so bad. I believe my partner Benny and I are the only scientists ever to explore what is in and under the sea. This book has been created for readers of all ages and levels of intelligence. Most of it, nevertheless, will go over your head. Forgive me if I find you bothersome.

There are many misconceptions about the ocean, generally perpetuated by the world's religions and poets. They will tell you that the sea is "angry" and "rough" and "foamy." These are myths that I will not bother to disprove. Have you seen the movie *Con Air*? Benny and I recently did, and enjoyed it a great deal. It was exciting but had heart.

The Haggis-on-Whey World of Unbelievable Brilliance is a series of books that explain the world, the universe, people, corporations, box making, and other untrustworthy entities. Because Benny and I are half-Scottish, our research is better than that done by Pakistanis, Chinese, Belgians, and the Swiss. None of those countries produce scientists worth their weight in meat.

People often complain about our books, which number 233 in total, and to these complainants I must direct my snorting laughter. Benny is in the basement, where he is tied to a pole, and he is laughing, too. We don't care about complainants.

What is in the ocean, you ask, besides water and tuna? The answer is not much. In researching this book, we spent many hours in the ocean, sometimes fully submerged, and we saw very little. This is why this book is slimmer than we had planned. If we discover more things in the ocean after the publication of this book, we will include it in subsequent printings. We will also post it on a web site. I am kidding.

One interesting thing about the sea that you will understand: anything you find in it can be eaten. This is different from trees or rocks or fire, and makes the ocean unique. If you put your hand in the ocean and pull something out, an animal or plant, you can put it straight into your mouth.

Yours truly,

Dr. Doris Haggis-on-Whey and Benny

SQUID HISTORY

Unlike giraffes, squids do not have a stupid history like arriving on Earth from space on a conveyor. They instead came from a normal place: the center of the Earth. Traveling through the same tunnels the molemen once used, the squids made the slow climb to the surface once the center of the Earth became played out. Many sociologists have discussed the rationale for this migration, citing such possible factors as food and darkness. However, the real answer is identity. The squids wanted to move to where the shakers and pushers were. At the time that place was the very, very far bottom of the ocean. Unfortunately, things have changed. The bottom of the ocean is a lot more subdued now. The mastodons and sharkmen have all moved away… and yet still the squids remain. Down in the dark, murky, dark waters, spending all their days swimming aimlessly. Swimming aimlessly and killing. And occasionally one of them glows in some neon color for a while. They're better than other animals of the ocean, though. I wish I could find my shoes. The soft ones I use for walking.

AM I BEING EATEN?

People get confused when they are being eaten. Sometimes they are not being eaten, but very often they are. A general rule of thumb is if you think you are being eaten, this is probably what is happening. Some questions to ask yourself:

1. ARE ANY OF MY LIMBS MISSING?

If there is a limb missing, and blood surrounding you, chances are an animal of the ocean has used its teeth to bite off part of your body. This means that you, or at least the part that was bitten off, is being eaten.

2. IS A BEAK-LIKE MOUTH EVISCERATING MY ORGANS?

This is the work of the giant squid, when it is eating you. The squid will use its tentacles to bring you into its orifice, then its razor-sharp beak will begin shredding your organs and liquefying your bones. These are signs you are being eaten.

3. AM I LIGHTHEADED AND ALSO DRINKING MY OWN BLOOD?

These are two common symptoms of being eaten. Often, when an animal is consuming your limbs, you lose a good deal of blood. This can cause lightheadedness. Also, when you are being pulled under the surface in the jaws or tentacles of an animal of the ocean, you will gulp water. And much of this water will be mixed with your own blood.

4. AM I INSIDE AN ANIMAL'S STOMACH?

If you find yourself inside a stomach, you have likely been eaten.

WHICH OF THESE MEN HAVE BEEN BITTEN BY A SEA CREATURE?

A   B   C   D   E   F

ANSWER: A-YES, B-YES, C-DON'T BE SILLY, D-YES, E-YES, F-YES

ORDER IN WHICH SQUIDS WILL EAT YOU	MALE, AVERAGE HEIGHT	WOMAN, AVERAGE HEIGHT	CHILDREN, ALL SIZES
	1. LEGS	1. ARMS	1. LEFT ARM, LEFT LEG
	2. ARMS	2. TORSO	2. LOWER TORSO
	3. HEAD	3. HEAD	3. RIGHT ARM, RIGHT LEG
	4. TORSO	4. LOWER TORSO	4. UPPER TORSO
	5. LOWER TORSO	5. LEGS	5. HEAD

FISH ARE ANIMALS AS ARE OTHER ANIMALS

Many biologists and teachers will claim that fish are not animals because they are shaped differently and have gills and are stupid. They want to relegate fish to second-class status because the brains of fish are smaller than those of wood chips or tulips. But this desire is motivated by factors outside of science. Here is a story that illustrates the problem:

A man walks up a mountain in the morning. In the afternoon, he climbs down the mountain. At night he stays in a lodge with a roaring fire and Belgian waffles. The next day, the fire has gone out and the Belgian waffles have been replaced by a golden retriever named Henry Fonda.

We know this story by heart, but too often we forget its simple message. And we do so at our peril. Fish are animals.

There is a movement afoot to pass laws to make fish animals in legal documents and plaques. Fill out the form opposite and send it to The Church of Latter-Day Saints, P.O. Box 71618, Poughkeepsie, NY, 12601.

DEAR PERSON,

The man in the mountain has a message for us all. Thank you for your patience.

_____   _____   _____
PRINT NAME   AGE   BENCH PRESS

_____
NUMBER OF FRUIT

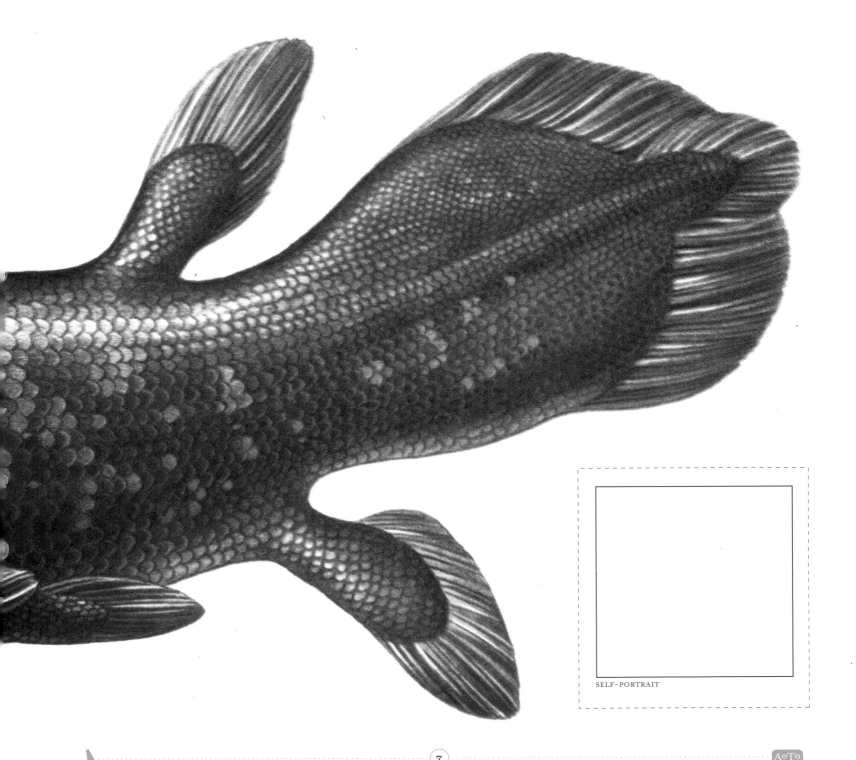

SELF-PORTRAIT

UNDERSTANDING THE GIANT SQUID

Some people say giant squids are difficult to locate, that they're very rare and possibly skittish. But really there are plenty of giant squids in the sea, and they are all social. They are, however, choosy. Some reasons why the best giant squids might be avoiding you:

- When you shake hands, you squeeze too soon, grabbing only fingertips.

- When the giant squid is telling a story, you constantly say, "Yeah" and "Uh-huh" in the middle of his sentences, instead of waiting until the end of a sentence to say "Yeah" or "Uh-huh".

- You keep talking about how good some skateboarder is at skateboarding, or how some other skateboarder isn't as good as some other skateboarder.

- You say things like "hang tough" and "vis-à-vis" and "apropos".

- You number the points you're about to make, though at least twice you've said, "I have three thoughts about that," when you've only had two.

SQUID DATING DOS AND DON'TS

For male squid:

Do Not make eye contact with your date

Do Not display anything made of silver, gold, or any light-reflecting alloy that might disturb your date's retinas

Do Not draw attention to your mouth, your eyes, your tentacles, or your personality

Do Not engage in any marveling, musing, or whimsical notioning

Do Not bring up Hobbes's notion of Natural Rights

Do Not eviscerate your date with your beak

Do Not offer your date ice cream, time shares, or a coupon for star registry

Do Not use the word "rendezvous"

Do Not offer your date literal or figurative "chill pills"

Do Not bring along Mark McGraff

For female squid:

Do thank your date for a lovely evening

DUTIES OF SQUID APPENDAGES

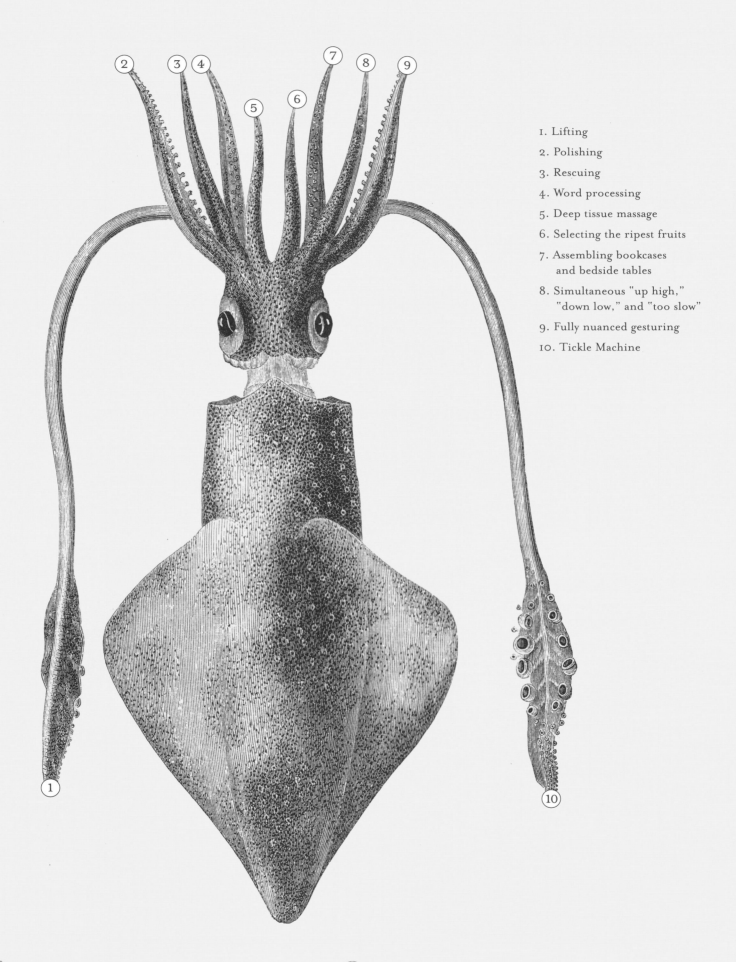

1. Lifting

2. Polishing

3. Rescuing

4. Word processing

5. Deep tissue massage

6. Selecting the ripest fruits

7. Assembling bookcases
   and bedside tables

8. Simultaneous "up high,"
   "down low," and "too slow"

9. Fully nuanced gesturing

10. Tickle Machine

BREAD AND THE OPEN SEA

There is no point in repeating the usual platitudes. Bread and the sea: it is a subject we will tackle here.

Many years ago, before bread, there was the sea. Then one day in the fifteenth century there was bread. Many people worried about the consequences of having both bread and the sea. And there was good reason to worry.

But now we are past all that. We live in a world where we no longer have to worry about rivalries and vengeance, at least as they pertain to bread and the sea. But will it always be this way? We have treaties, and strong nets, and the one wall, but is it enough? Some would say it is not enough.

But what can we do? We cannot live in fear. We cannot hide in our shelters or wear dark cloaks and thigh-high boots. We have to go on living. We have to ride our bicycles and fly our kites and tie our friends in the shed with rope and duct tape. We have to live. There may come a day when the sea and bread find a way to again bring their differences to our front porch. It could be tomorrow. Or next year. You could be dead by that time. But if you are not dead, you could be at work, drinking soda and writing words on paper—or typing them. And then the sound of conflict will come into your ears, accompanied by a bright light, and the unmistakable heat of eternal fire.

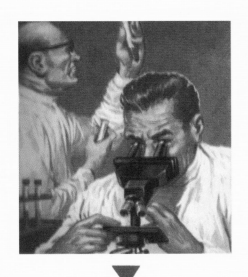

HOW BREAD IS MADE

WHY IS IT SO DARK IN THE DARK PART OF THE SEA?

There are many theories about this. We will explore none of them. We will explore only one of them. Here is the theory we will explore, which is fact because I am telling you it. The dark part of the sea is very dark because the sea is surrounded by heavy velvet curtains, which are meant to keep out the light. The sea got this idea from a man named Greg, who was the ringmaster of a circus that performed late at night, mostly in the Plains States. Greg wouldn't get home until 2 o'clock in the morning most days, and to sleep a proper amount he had to buy some very heavy velvet curtains, the color of blood, to keep out the sun and make his bedroom seem night-like. One day the sea came to see Greg's circus, which was a terrible circus where panthers spoke too quickly and all the rings weren't round but oval. They got to talking afterward, and Greg passed on the idea of the dark curtains. The sea asked where Greg got his dark curtains, and Greg said he got them at Bed Bath and Beyond, but Pottery Barn had even nicer ones, if the sea's budget wasn't too tight. The sea wasn't sure what kind of budget it had for the curtains, but would run some numbers and figure it out. The sea liked to run numbers on its watch, which doubled as a calculator. So later that night, the sea did some calculating on its wristwatch, and figured it could spend the money for the nicer curtains. The next day, the sea bought enough navy-blue velvet curtains to cover all the deeper parts of the ocean, and that's why the sea is very dark in the parts where it's dark, but it doesn't explain the smell.

TYPES OF DUMB DOLPHINS

BROWN ONES

PINK AMAZON ONES

SICK ONES

PACKS OF DOLPHINS

DOLPHINS THAT
SAVE PEOPLE

DOLPHINS THAT LET
YOU PET THEM

DOLPHINS THAT
RIDE WAVES

DOLPHINS THAT LOOK
LIKE THEY'RE SMILING

GREY ONES

SQUID INK LEAVES ITS MARK

Squid ink, known for its permanence and viscosity, has played a key role in many moments of historical significance throughout history:

- In 1515 the Man of Gravistade signed the Document of Agreement Treaty using a 36-ounce solid-pewter pen dipped in squid ink. The Man of Gravistade was well known for his beard, which is featured in a nursery rhyme still chanted in the halls of Montessori schools today: "Sixty-seven years long, why wear pants at all? (why wear pants at all?)"

THE ONLY KNOWN RENDERING
OF THE RECLUSIVE TAILOR, KLARN

- The first napkin sketch of the auto-theft-prevention device and rhythm clave known as "The Club" was penned using a squid-ink ballpoint.

- The frock coat of Vice President Alben Barkley, worn the night of the 1951 Refinery Ball (the same evening of the Vice President's tar-pit mumble), was hand-sewn by Klarn, a Washington tailor so famous for his creative use of squid dyes that he outgrew his need for a last name.

- The footprints on the birth certificate of Morten Hacket, the celebrated singer and maker of fine boots, were printed off a stamp pad of squid ink.

- Prince Hans Tandy Small lost 3.5 pounds in just eight hours after ingesting a spoonful of squid ink and pig butter, a fashionable 19th-century skin salve not designed to be administered orally.

- The shadow behind the governmental crest of authenticity featured on the lower-left corner on the back of the current 5,000-lira bill was inspired by a woman who kept squid ink in her closet, next to her silver box full of silver bells.

- The pewter chalice used on opening night of *Sing Your Life (The Musical)* was polished to a sheen (one critic described it as "glaring") using a squid-ink paste and the hands of toddler twins from Bonn.

- The distracting squalls of Charles Dickens's third child, who was chronically chapped, were quelled with drops of squid ink mixed into the infant's bottle, which caused the child to fall into a silent stupor, thereby allowing the author to complete his final editing pass of *Bleak House*.

- The paint painter René Magritte used to create the pipe in his notable "Ceci n'est pas une Pipe" (translation: "Put that near your pipes and toast it") has been tested by a computer and revealed to be 100% squid ink.

WHO WAS RENÉ MAGRITTE?

Painter René Magritte was an artist who painted pictures on canvas and sometimes on paper. And sometimes on board, or heavy paper. The paintings that René Magritte painted were considered very funny in his time, but now are considered very serious. They are considered so serious that they have inspired many credos and some aphorisms.

LESSER KNOWN WORKS BY RENÉ MAGRITTE

"Ceci n'est pas une Boutonniere"
"Ceci n'est pas une Coup D'Etat"
"My bad, c'est una Pipe"

WORLD'S TALLEST GIANT SQUID

The first thing a person notices about giant squid is how tall they are. Almost everyone comments on their height, which is tall. In 1970, a team of sailors and nautical scholars witnessed a giant squid close to thirty feet in height, a record that remained unchallenged until 2003, when a middle-school teacher reportedly encountered a fifty-footer while monitoring a "See, Hear, Taste, Swim" field trip off the coast of Austria. Over the course of my own research, I have chanced upon giant squid well over seventy-five feet tall. I have even observed an entire giant-squid family trying on shoes in a discount clothing outlet, and the shortest among them was one hundred and twenty feet tall. As underwater photography is considered gauche, I have no visual proof of the sighting, but because science is based on trust, in lieu of photos I give you this drawing. I like the colors and the way the ocean is green and foamy.

HOW TALL IS THE WORLD'S TALLEST GIANT SQUID?

It's taller than the world's tallest novelty screwdriver below, middle. At right is Ed Asner.

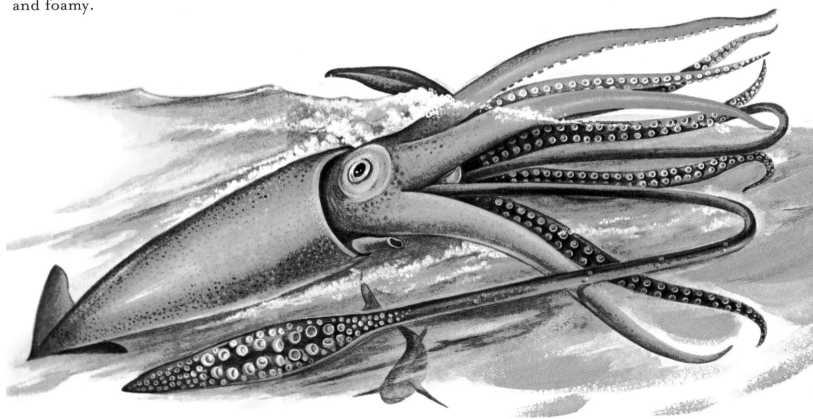

WHAT DOES A SQUID EAT IN AN AVERAGE DAY?

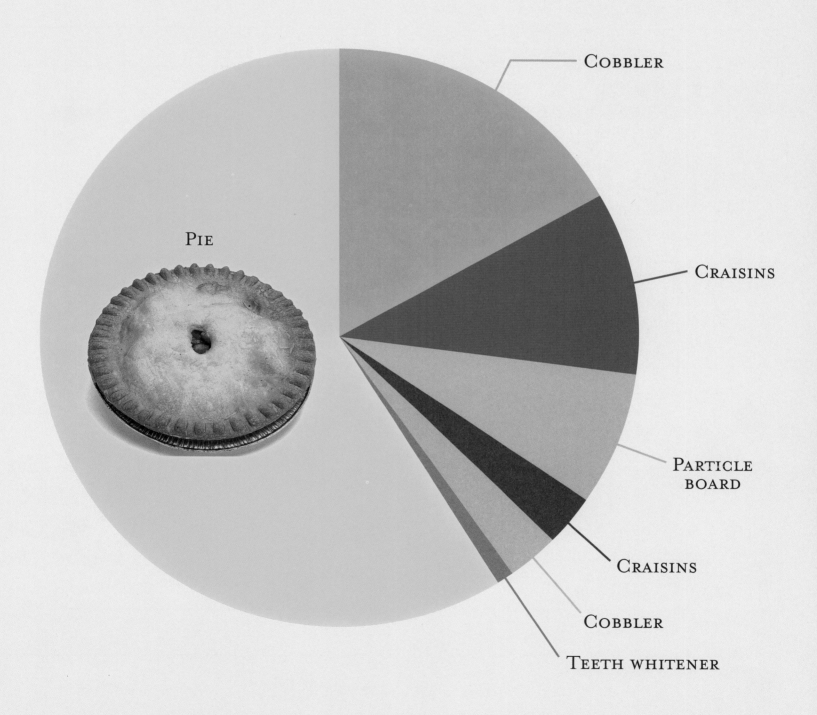

Cobbler

Craisins

Pie

Particle Board

Craisins

Cobbler

Teeth whitener

TYPICAL SQUID MEALS AND THE

BREAKFAST	1/2 Grapefruit 2 bowls Kellogg's Fruit Harvest with Real Peaches w/ 6 oz. 2% Milk 600 lbs of Drowned Polar Bear 1 8 oz. Dannon Fruit on the Bottom Yogurt (Blackberry)

LUNCH	2 cups Campbell's Tomato Soup 1 10 oz. glass V8 juice cocktail 2 cups of Coffee (Black) 1 severed sailor's arm 1 Blue Whale (small)

SNACK	3/4 of female partner's offspring (approx. 4,600 oz.) 1 0.3 lb bag of red seedless grapes 1 salted Auntie Anne's pretzel

DINNER	1 medium-sized Settlement of Emperor Penguins (no beaks) 1 container French Fries (air-baked, not fried) 1 1/2 lb Caesar Salad 1 2 oz. Low-Fat Hidden Valley Caesar Dressing 25 schools of Porcupine Pufferfish (*Didion holacanthus*)
DESSERT	3 scoops of person's head

MIDNIGHT SNACK	2 16 oz. bags of Lay's KC Masterpiece BBQ Flavored Potato Chips 0.35 lb bowl of "Ants-on-a-Log" (traditional PBR style) 1 Deep-Sea-Rescue Volunteer Team (w/ wetsuits)

CORRESPONDING DIETARY ANALYSIS

Analysis: Milk and yogurt come from cows and goats, and in most cases, squids would prefer just to eat the cows or goats. When squids eat cows and goats, they squeeze them with their tentacles, then eviscerate them with their beaks, going for the stomach area first. Sometimes, for fun, squids will first pretend to milk the cow or goat. But that is only when there are other squids around who will appreciate the joke.

Analysis: Coffee has been a problem with the squid. Coffee provides a jolt in the late morning, when the energy of the squid tends to lag. But squids do not like the taste of coffee, because coffee does not taste good. For some time, squids used a good deal of sugar to mask the bland and ham-like taste of coffee. This did not work. But then the squids discovered Sweet and Low, which seemed to be able to cut through the ham and sweeten the drink. Tables from Ikea break.

Analysis: Squids are inclined toward diabetes, so this is too much sodium for a squid.

Analysis: This is probably too much dairy. A typical squid knows that it is too much dairy, but they like dairy products. They like the color of cream. It is a white color, but a three-dimensional whiteness that has no equal in nature. Or perhaps only the beluga whale can equal the whiteness of cream. Beluga whales are delicious, if they are eviscerated right.

Analysis: It is strange when you are a squid and you eat people wearing wetsuits. The rubber taste is hard to get out of one's beak. Some squids will follow wetsuit with tomato juice or cashews, but this does not always work. A good thing to do with a hat is to put it on top of another hat.

PREPARING FOR YOUR DIVE

Before you explore the dark and cold waters of the deep, in fact before you even feel the sand of the beach between your toes, there are things to do. First you need plenty of brown fat. Brown fat is a layer of blubber, typically stored just beneath the skin, which keeps its owner warm and dry and satisfied when it comes time to dive. A good layer of brown fat can take up to seven years and a great deal of mayonnaise to generate. Snacks are also a must, as is a good pocketknife, one with scissors. A warm bathing suit is good, as is a deep-sea detector. Other optional items include: a pocket mirror; a translation dictionary; hard candy for trading; a book of famous toasts and quotes.

WHERE ARE THE UNPREPARED NOW?

DIVER	FATE
DON, UNPREPARED IN 1988	BECAME VERY COLD
HELEN, UNPREPARED IN 1990	BECAME VERY COLD
ICHIRO, UNPREPARED IN '87, '93	PRESUMED CHEWED INTO BLOODY PULP OF UNPREPAREDNESS
TOM R., UNPREPARED IN 1985	BECAME COLD
DAWN, UNPREPARED IN '69, '91, '03	BECAME COLD EACH TIME

2006 HOLIDAY CALENDAR FOR THE CENTRAL GOVERNMENT OFFICES OF THE DEEP (RESTRICTED):

INDEPENDENCE DAY, JANUARY 12

THE FLOATING HOLIDAYS, MAY 11

CLEAN WATER ACT, JUNE 19

EYE SAFETY WEEK, AUGUST 12-19

LUMINESCENCE, APRIL 27

ROPE AND LADDER DAY, JUNE 14

THE CONCEPTION, JUNE 30

LUNG NIGHT, DECEMBER 15

DEFINING THE DEEP: THE ELEVEN LAYERS OF THE SEA AND THEIR DIFFERENT NAMES AND FEATURES

There are many layers or zones in the ocean. These all have names, just as you have a name and many Portugese have names. Each of these layers is distinct and many of them are different colored. I am the first to name these layers and this is the first time these names are in print.

LAYER ONE: "THE TOP LAYER"
This is the layer where the sun comes through and gets glittery.

LAYER TWO: "THE NEXT LAYER"
Here is where they test combustible engines and crossbows.

LAYER THREE: "THE THIRD LAYER"
This is mostly tract housing.

LAYER FOUR: "THE LAYER DEDICATED TO EXCELLENCE"
This layer is dedicated to excellence.

LAYER FIVE: "THE MAIN LAYER"
This is where the animals of the ocean emit feces and then swim among their feces.

LAYER SIX: "THE LAYER BELOW THE ONE WITH THE FECES"

This layer has less feces than the one above it, but a lot of feces still drift down here, which makes this a layer a bad place to live.

LAYER SEVEN: "THE LAYER WITH NO NAME"

This layer wishes it was the layer below it.

LAYER EIGHT: "ANOTHER LAYER WITH NO NAME"

This layer is colder and still has feces in it. There have been complaints.

LAYER NINE: "THE LAYER THEY CALL MICKEY"

This is where they misuse the word "apropos".

LAYER TEN: "THE SCOTCH-IRISH LAYER"

No one in this layer has read *Ulysses*.

LAYER ELEVEN: "AT LAST, THIS LAYER"

Most of the interesting animals spend their time here. Squids. Giant squids. Animals eaten by squids and giant squids. Animals with dial-up internet service. Animals wearing estate jewelry. Animals who braid each other's hair while talking about what water feels like to the fishes.

SO MUCH PRESSURE

The pressure at the bottom of the ocean is many times greater than it is on land. The pressure is powerful enough to crush submarines and statues. It has been known to make undersea divers do certain things, like hug too long. Fish of the ocean, which have lived in the sea most of their lives, have developed a number of ways to cope with the pressure. Smart divers know these tricks. If you are a stupid diver, and most divers are stupid, then read.

• Visualize the tips of your toes relaxing, then visualize the bottoms of your feet relaxing, then visualize the bumps of bone on the sides of your ankles relaxing, then visualize the long thing that attaches your heel to your leg relaxing, then visualize the loose caps of your knees relaxing, then visualize all your pale middle parts relaxing, then visualize your scalp relaxing, and your jaw, and your cheeks, and your eyelids, and your gums, and your dirty unworthy fingers that have done harm to all they have touched.

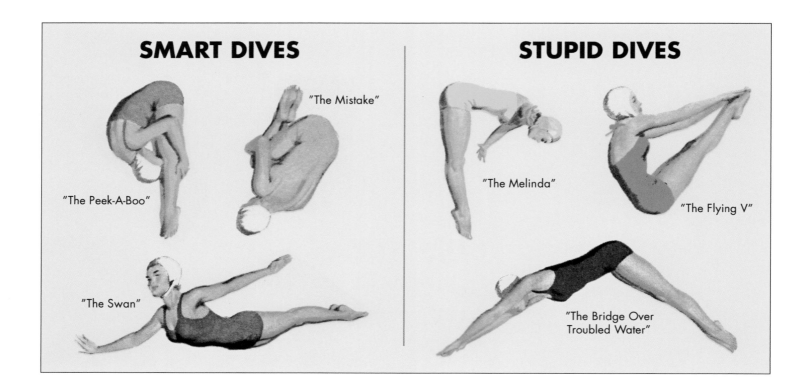

SMART DIVES

"The Mistake"

"The Peek-A-Boo"

"The Swan"

STUPID DIVES

"The Melinda"

"The Flying V"

"The Bridge Over Troubled Water"

• Puzzles. An unfinished puzzle is the badge of uncertainty, and uncertainty stinks of weakness, and pressure feeds on the fatty meats of weakness.

• Picture yourself floating in a dark, cold, unforgiving ocean. Then picture Benny and myself sitting by a roaring fire in head-to-toe fleece, laughing and drinking hot drinks.

• Buy a small rectangular tray about 11 inches long and 9 inches wide and 3 inches high and fill it with sand and smooth rocks. Experiment with placing the rocks in different areas of the tray. Trace patterns in the sand with your fingers. Fill your hand with sand and clasp your hand in a fist and let the sand stream slowly out from the bottom of your fist. Move the tray to a quiet corner and leave the room, making sure the door shuts firmly behind you.

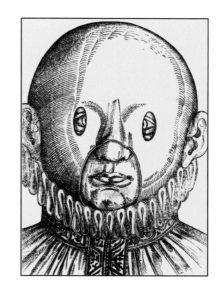

• Hats have been proven to have sedative effects. Hats on top of hats are doubly good, but sometimes inspire envy. When one inspires envy, treachery is often close behind. After treachery, there is often pilates.

FRED THE MANATEE WHO GREW A LOOK

At age 10 Fred decided he wanted a look so he set about trying to get one. By age 12 he thought he had a look but he did not. People thought he looked confused and ambiguous. His look was not right. By age 14 Fred thought his look was pronounced. Combining many styles already seen with a few flourishes on his part Fred was confident that he now had a look. The truth was he did not. This realization came with laughter and a great deal of it. For the next couple years Fred imitated people with certain looks that hung out in groups with other people with that same look. However, he did not execute this imitation very well and they did not accept that his look resembled their look. That was frustrating. And yet, one day Fred woke up at the age of 18 and he had it. The look was his after years of careful cultivation. He went to concerts, parties, and sporting events sporting his look. People with a look like his look welcomed him in. Now he and they formed a group, a group with a look. That was 1994, the year Dakota Fanning came into our world.

WHAT DOES WATER DO ON WEEKENDS?

Water is restless. Water is petulant. Water is passive-aggressive and unhappy at parties. But water is also hard-working, and Monday through Friday, we know that water is busy, wreaking havoc on shoreline property and drowning merchant marines. What most people don't know is what water does on Friday night, on sunny Saturday, and on holy Sunday. One thing water does not do is talk about his mother. Something about water's mother makes water tense, so mother is a subject he avoids. His family in general—he does not like to talk about his family. He does not like to talk or think about horses or Congress or knives or the Falklands. On weekends, he prefers to pretend he can draw. He will go down to the art-supply store, buy a new pad of paper and some charcoal, and invite a friend over to pose. Then he will draw for an hour, after which time he is convinced anew that he cannot draw. He will send his friend home. He will go into the garage and will try to build a table. He will avoid thinking about his mother. He will hammer away at the table and not think about his family. He will then go to the pet store to look for a puppy. He will name all the puppies at the pet store, with names like Nils, Nigel, Basil, Rupert, but will take none of them home. He will call up an old girlfriend, the one who liked the same music, ragtime, as he did. She will suddenly sound too much like his mother and he will hang up. Finally, he will take some carrot sticks and go into the basement to carve shoes. Water's family was originally from Holland, which is located near the Netherlands and just below where the Dutch live, and all the water of Holland is taught at a young age about the therapeutic benefits of carving shoes on weekends. The best kind of wood to use when carving shoes is oak.

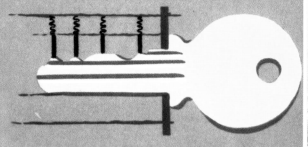

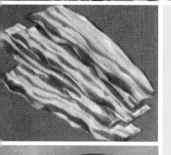

HOW WATER SPENT
LAST SATURDAY

(CLOCKWISE FROM UPPER LEFT)

1. MADE NEW KEYS TO SHED
2. WENT TO PARADE IN NEXT TOWN
3. CHOPPED DOWN HISTORICAL OAK
   TREE IN NEIGHBOR'S YARD
4. DUSTED CROPS
5. SCREENED FILMS BY BUÑUEL
6. BACON TIME
7. MEASURED ALMOST EVERYTHING

AN UNDERWATER STORY...
THAT OCCURRED IN SIOUX CITY

Wobbegongs are large, ugly, catfish-looking animals that tend to troll the bottom of the shallow coasts for crabs and sea snails. They are not aggressive but they are equipped with razor-sharp teeth and a suctioning mouth that is capable of hanging on to larger prey for hours at a time. These mundane facts were solely of interest to one R.J. Cornucopia, who, one unfortunate morning, found one firmly attached to his stomach. Not only was the fish firmly attached despite all shakes and squirms on R.J.'s part, but the animal was also proudly protruding its full 0.8 meters perpendicularly off R.J.'s body. In spite of this, R.J. attempted to persevere and began dressing for school. However, as he put on his new striped button-down, he noticed his new acquaintance was making his fine shirt lose the shape of its fine Italian cut.

"This will never do," said a dismayed R.J. Cornucopia. He pondered, Maybe if I reason with this animal, it might let go. And so, with the help of a protractor, a wet sponge, and a brief PowerPoint presentation, R.J. attempted to illustrate to his new anatomical ancillary the merits of releasing itself from his stomach and once again enjoying their lives separately. There was no reaction.

R.J. made the next logical move and began poking the wobbegong repeatedly in the eye. The fish merely shrugged. What kind of fish is this? The wobbegong did not respond to this line of questioning, so R.J. marched off to the local library to find out the answer for himself. *Eucrossorhinus dasypogon,* or wobbegong. "Well fancy that!" said R.J. As he continued to read he felt a sharp pain in his stomach. It appeared that while he was reading, the wobbegong had begun chewing into R.J.'s flesh. Young Cornucopia grimaced and ran the fish into a nearby bookcase. The fish still held. "Well," sighed R.J. "I guess I'm just going to have to get used to this thing." He left the library and returned home on his bike. However, just as R.J. began envisioning his new life with a member of the *Orectolobidae* forcibly wedded to his abdomen, a funny thing happened. He walked inside and his entire family and friends yelled, "Surprise!" "Happy flagpole day!" they shouted. He stood confused. The fish blinked. "You see, R.J., that fish we got was

part of your big flagpole-day surprise. Great, huh?" R.J. admitted that it was pretty amusing. After eating some of his cake, R.J. asked how they planned to remove the punch line from his lower torso. "Oh no, that's your present. That stays."

R.J. did not argue with his family, because he was weak-willed and thirsty. He got himself some mineral water and sat down.

THE HAGGIS-ON-WHEY WORLD OF CUTTLEFISH

SEVEN CAUTIONARY TALES ABOUT OCTOPUSES AND OTTERS

GARY

There was an otter named Gary. He was sad because he wanted to be a giant squid, but did not have the money for the operation. He later married unhappily and sold printer cartridges. The end.

ANNALISA

This one otter was female so she was called Annalisa. She lived in Ames, Iowa. She had four children who she had forgotten to name. The children didn't care, because they figured one day they would be eaten by an orca. This happened on Thursday.

DENNY

He was a truck driver and also an octopus. He wanted to have the operation to make himself a giant squid, and he had the money to do it. But on the day of the operation, he was drafted into the army and was sent to Lisbon. There he became involved with masons and jazz dancers and was not heard from again. Until some time later, when he went back to driving a truck. In a different part of Portugal.

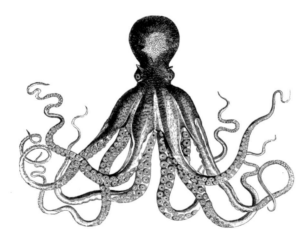

THERESA

This was a very old octopus whose real name was Strom Thurmond. The end.

FIDELIO

There was a time when all the otters were naming their sons Fidelio.

IGNACIO

The itch he couldn't scratch was no itch at all. Another good movie is *M*A*S*H*.

REBECCA

There are times when I think this name sounds harsh. Does it sound like being slapped? Sometimes it does, to me. She was a fiery one, this octopus named Rebecca. She carried a violin case everywhere with her, for she wanted people to think she was a violinist. She was not a violinist. She played no stringed instruments. Inside her violin case was not a violin, but a muskrat. And inside the muskrat was a heart, a stomach, some veins, and some blood. The muskrat had no name because he had been raised by otters.

NOISES IN THE EAR: A DIAGNOSTIC FLOW CHART

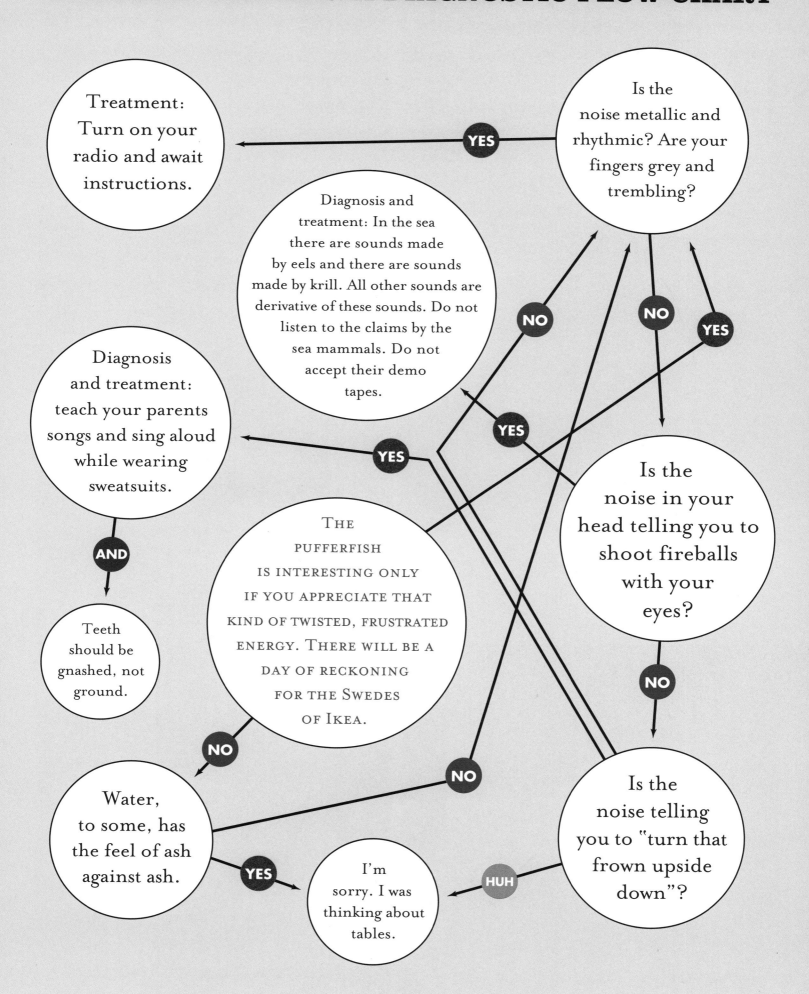

FISH AND ARMS

Every school child is taught that until recently, fish had arms. There have been rumors circulating for a long time that all of the fish lost their arms in thresher accidents, but this is only partly true. They did lose their arms suddenly, but it was not on a farm. It was somewhere else. The fish also used to have hair. Impressive hair. All of the fish of the ocean had magnificent hair of every kind, and they were very proud of this hair. They would comb it, and perm it, and gel it, and sometimes make people smell it. But one day something happened to all their hair, and that something was named Reggie Theus. Most people know Reggie Theus as a former professional basketball player who now does commentary for NBA broadcasts, but most people don't know that Mr. Theus harbored a secret hatred of the great hair worn by fish. So one day he set out to make all of the fish hairless, and this is why most fish appear to be bald. Just how Reggie Theus accomplished this is a story for another day. It's also in the Bible.

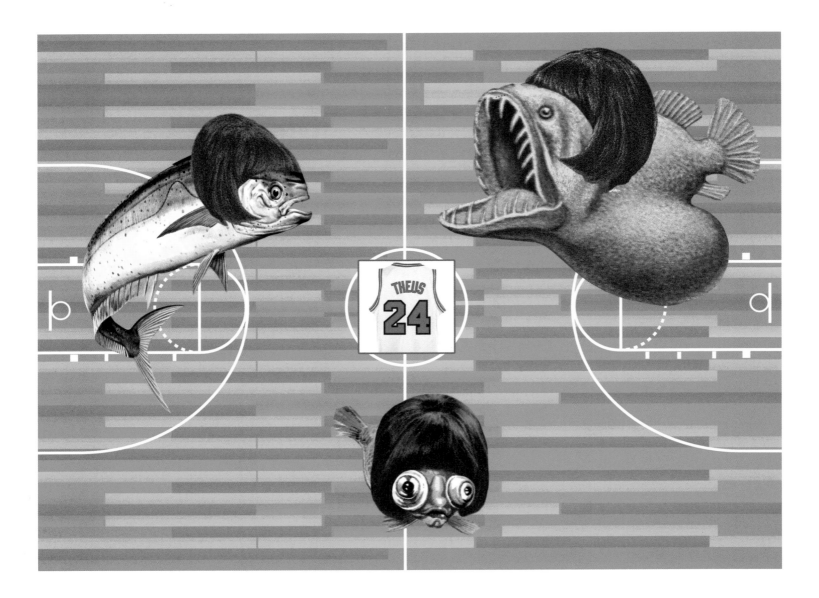

SHARK RELIGION: AT A GLANCE

Unlike our own religions, the religion of sharks is based primarily on where little marbles land in small concave holes on a wooden board.

Like in South-Northern religions, sacred religious documents are stored on thin slices of Columbus dry salami.

The religion's sacred months are April through January. The rest are holy.

Newborns are inducted into the religion through a ritual in which they are lacquered with oil and then lacquered with jelly and then lacquered with lacquer.

The most pious sharks in the religion are rewarded with neckties and papal bobblehead dolls. The unpious are prohibited from competing in all freestyle skate-offs and are not given neckties.

There are a lot of barbecues.
No women or girls or other deviants are permitted.

If a brother of the religion ever finds himself with an excess of mohair, he is expected to extend a bucket of it to his fellow brother for the betterment of his brother's scarecrow-family miniseries.

There are no candles or stained glass in shark religion, but there is braised brisket.
This is worn around the neck.

Shark priests do not sanction shark weddings. That is done by the sheriff.

CAN I KEEP HIM? A GUIDE TO GIANT SQUID OWNERSHIP

Keeping a giant squid as a pet or medical aide is ill-advised. Captivity makes them paranoid and judgmental. But if you're set on the idea, and you have extra room at home or in your medical office, there are guidelines that will prevent the squid from dying or from eating your head.

- Giant squids are not punctual. Hassling them about this might enrage them. When squids are enraged, they eat flesh and make sweeping statements.

- Giant squids will try to steal your friends, wooing them with charm bracelets and fresh bread. They also might eviscerate your friends with their beaks.

- Giant squids are nosy: anyone who comes knocking when a giant squid is around—boyfriends, trick-or-treaters, exterminators—can expect the third degree. They also might eviscerate your visitors with their beaks.

- When you are doing major surgery, squids can be useful if you enunciate your needs clearly and pay on time.

- Cover electrical outlets.

- Hide small toys.

- Deal with all problems in an upfront manner. Squids value forthrightness above all. If they feel they are being undermined there will be tension.

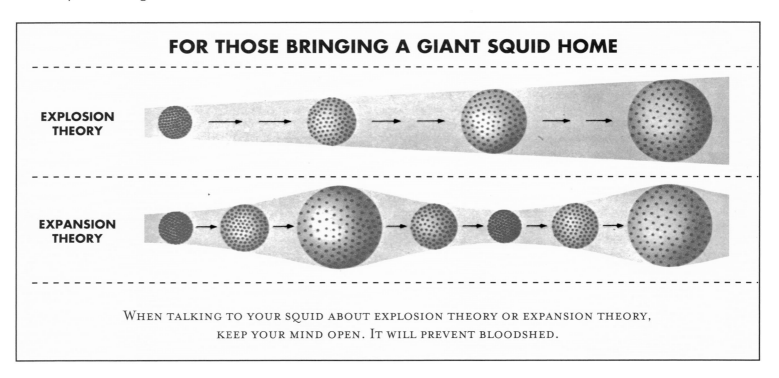

FOR THOSE BRINGING A GIANT SQUID HOME

EXPLOSION THEORY

EXPANSION THEORY

When talking to your squid about explosion theory or expansion theory, keep your mind open. It will prevent bloodshed.

SQUID TRENDS AND FASHIONS

WEST COAST	**DIRTY SOUTH**
Curvy and top-water tan	Undernourished and deep-sea pale
Backpack, both shoulders	Backpack, one shoulder
Suctioning	Squeezing
Royal blue with red piping	Navy blue with red piping
Books as accessories	Babies as accesories
Fold-over sandwich baggies	Zip-lock sandwich baggies
Layering	Cuffing
Saving ink to hone focus and control	Squirting whenever the mood strikes
Tall, skinny bookshelves	Short, wide bookshelves
Winking	Elaborate handshakes
Flying kites	Picnics

MOST POPULAR BABY NAMES

ANIMAL	PICTURE	BOYS	GIRLS
Sea Horse		Michael	Alexis
Stingray		Michael, Keith	Alexis
Ribbonfish		Tyler	Olivia
Swordfish		Dylan	Mackensie/Makenzie
John Dory		Brandon	Jordan
Mackerel		Brandon	Trinity
Silverside		Austin	Sierra
Thresher Shark		Caleb	Dakota
Moonfish		Cody	Bailey
Spiny-headed Worm		Noah, Cody	Miranda
Sperm Whale		Mason	Cheyenne
Flatworm		Elijah	Sabrina
Killer Whale		Kyle	Angel
Tongue Worm		Elijah	Kiara
Snakehead		Cameron	Kennedy
Gastrotrich		Trevor	Chloe
Carp		Cody	Autumn
Jellyfish		Aidan	Skylar/Skyler
Crab		Dakota	Destiny
Dolphin		Bryce	Aaliyah/Aliyah
Salmon		Colby	Tatiana
Basking Shark		Alec	Ariel
Ray's Bream		Colton	Delaney
Prawn		Omar	Dana
Flying Fish		Jose	Reagan

FOR FIFTY SELDOM SEEN SEA ANIMALS

ANIMAL	PICTURE	BOYS	GIRLS
Halibut		Brady	India
Hatchetfish		Preston	Raven
Catfish		Dustin	Ruby
Rabbitfish		Chandler	Dakota
Mussel		Taylor	Cheyenne
Pufferfish		Cody	Genesis
Little Post-Horn Squid		Cody	Brooklyn
Octopus		Damian	Judaica
Fu Manchu		Dawson	Asia
Giant Squid		Andre	Guantanamo/Guantanama
Eel		Shane	Mercedes
Sea Urchin		Derek	Dakota
Squid		Travis	Hope
Snipe Eel		Noah	Condoleeza
Dirty Phish Fan		Cody	Dakota
Lobster		Cody	Cheyenne
Big-Headed Rattail		Chestnut	Richard
Wonder-lamp Squid		Brady	Apple
Oarfish		Jordache	Tangelo
Batfish		Cody	Dakota
Lazy Squid		Parker	South Dakota
Pelican Eel		Henry/Henri	Addison
Devilfish		Michael	State
Starfish		Elijah	Wacker
Lanternfish		Frodo	Michigan

MUSICAL THEATER AT SEA

For a deep understanding of the sea, a researcher must submerge herself in its culture. Unfortunately, full submersion in sea life means sitting through a great deal of musical theater. Musicals lie at the heart of all important aspects of sea life. Typical get-to-know-you conversation in the sea begins with, "What's your favorite?" as in "What is your favorite musical?" Not having a ready answer reveals a researcher as ignorant and potentially undateable. Business, pleasure, medical examinations—all significant discoveries and decisions unfold while the creatures of the deep watch *Mary Dreams Alone* or *The Guns Go Woo* or one of the other many big-name shows of the sea. If you plan on spending time in the ocean, even just an afternoon skim-boarding, it is imperative that you familiarize yourself with the basic plots and characters of the sea's most famous musicals:

DOG DAYS A "musical within a musical," *Dog Days* begins when the beautiful Maribel, dancing and singing star of *The Lederhosen of October*, accidentally breaks her collarbone and canine talent "Diggy" must fill in at the last minute. Octoberfest turns into Dogtoberfest as misunderstandings and romance bloom offstage and on, and the show opens to surprise rave reviews. Famous for sing-along classics such as "Yes, I'm Not Married," "Roll Over With Me," and "Why (Not)?"

THE GUNS GO WOO Poor yet talented gun maker Gere toils by day in the gun factory while at night he crafts gorgeous custom firearms. Gere's destiny of obscurity and toil takes an unexpected turn when Dana, daughter of gun factory owner Rene, disguises herself as a man and unwittingly ignites a bar brawl, earning herself a glimpse of the Innkeeper's gun, an impressive example of Gere's handiwork. Dana spends all of Act Two discovering the identity of the illusive gun maker. Act Three she discovers love. Featuring "A Bullet for Every Gun," "Trigger Happy," and "Shake, Jump, Kneel, and Sigh."

PAINT MISBEHAVIN'! Every night, painter Reese works on a portrait of a beautiful woman, a woman whom he has never met. The painting gets more detailed each day until the woman of the painting becomes so real that she bursts into song. The next morning, Reese brags of his new love to his friends, but when they return to his studio, she remains a mute, lifeless painting. It is only by painting himself next to her in the portrait that Reese is able to truly sing with her. With hits such as "Tomorrow Something Great's Gonna Happen," "Yellow, Nice to Meet You," and "Blue Who?"

A CAROLE EDDY PRODUCTION

SWIMMING OUT LOUD

THE TUBEWORM: RAINBOW OF EMOTION

With no mouth, no stomach, and no arms to communicate with, the tubeworm can seem aloof. But this is not so. Learn to read the subtle body language of the tubeworm.

EMOTION	CAUSED BY	APPEARANCE
Happiness	Marvin Gaye	
Sorrow	Flower bed crushed by escaping robbers	
Rage	Midsection poked repeatedly	
Embarrassment	Torn pants	
Hooray!	Big raise	
A HA!	Crime solved	
Deep and profound love	Teresa R.	

THE SUBMARINE RADIO:
AN INSTRUMENT OF IMPORTANCE

A sea submarine is made up of many important parts. The steering stick is key, and the propeller is also considered crucial. Then there are the floaters, and the fin trimming, and also the paint. But the most important part of a submarine is the sea radio. Submarine radios are very delicate instruments, capable of picking up sea-horse conversations from a distance of thirty nautical yards, or a miscalculation deep inside a stingray's brain. And yet submarine microphones are also sturdy things, able to withstand crushing pressures, cold water, and certain clothing. But not all sea noise appeals to the submarine radio. Some noises—the talk of children, the scrubbing of tubs and sinks—make sea-submarine radios tense. Other sounds, such as rhythmic snapping, sanding, lifting, decay, and moisturizing, give it great pleasure. It is not important, however, that sea-submarine radios are kept content. Most scientists believe that any number of asteroids are right now hurtling toward the Earth, rendering mundane concerns about happiness irrelevant. I wish you Final Days of relief and little chafing.

THINGS NEEDED FOR UNDERWATER EXPLORATION

Underwater exploration is not easy, but with some preparation, you can do it. Below are guidelines and requirements that will make it possible to investigate some of the intriguing legends of the sea.

THE FORGOTTEN CAVE OF PRINCE MERMANADOR

Myth: Ancient underwater lore tells the tale of a walk the beloved prince took on the day he was to be crowned. As he entered his favorite cave to collect his thoughts, his jealous cousin assassinated him and fed his body to a school of eels, leaving only his goblet and sword of power hidden somewhere deep in this now-cursed underwater locale.

What You'll Need: A PhD in oceanography and nautical archaeology and $40 million.

THE GOLDEN DIAMOND MINE OF GORBALOO

Myth: A freak convergence of the rarest of earthly minerals, this marvel of lore is rumored to contain such magnificently gorgeous beauty that a mere glance inside the cave could render an explorer sightless and blind.

What You'll Need: A PhD in oceanography and geophysics, and a graduate degree in maritime history. And $80 million.

THE MAGICAL SUNKEN VIKING WARSHIP OF THORD THORSTEIN

Myth: Before crossing the Atlantic for the first time, the vikings sent mighty sailor Thord Thorstein to clear the path of unwanted pirates and sea marauders. However, Thord and his crew were swallowed by a Leviathan who coveted their furry shoes.

What You'll Need: PhDs in Nordic culture, ocean engineering, nautical exploration, thermodynamics, and string theory. And an initial deposit of $190 million.

ANCIENT MARINER SEA RHYME

(As Reinterpreted either by Fred, by a squid named Fred, or by Fred, the squid named Fred)

Har, ye big boats of sea unto waves... doth passing!
Arrgh garrh, ye doom is mine dessert,
Thine festoons do not mightily billow enough says I,
Gnar dagar! Me thinks me hungry massively.
Is it cool if I eat your deckhand while we talk?

Hooray! The full moon! Blesser and keeper of the deep's keepsakes
For 'tis come the arrival of the welcoming of great Dirk, the returned,
Having returned
Raise thy goblets of fire, o mine brethren,
And also other spectating fish...
I really wish I could stop crying

Brotherhood of men!
Boatpeople of whom I address
While ye drink of the mythic elixir of life and also juice
Remember me... No, forget about me
Ignore me, truthfully
And while thou dance the dance of kings
I'll wait over here and sneak up and stuff,
And end your life.

THE STRIKING FISH COAL MINERS OF OCEANIA

In the 1960s, fish coal miners had no rights. They had basic rights but not the kind of rights fish coal miners want. Throughout the years, the coal mining boss told them, "I'm not going to pay you fish coal miners another cent." And because the boss was from Iowa, the fish coal miners knew he meant it. And so the fish coal miners did the only thing fish coal miners know how to do: they stroked... struck. They went on strike. But the boss held firm, citing many reasons why he would not cave in: rising cost of benefits, low stock value, a lack of any underwater coal to mine, and worker tardiness. But the fish coal miner strike leader said that was just another ruse from the craven boss. "We've heard all that before," said the fish coal miner strike leader. His name was Doug. "He always tells us, 'Why should I pay you so much when there isn't even any coal to mine or even a coal mine to mine in?' Well, I ask you, why did you buy us coal carts and pickaxes? If there're no shafts to crawl into every day to blacken my fish lungs, then why I am wearing a miner's helmet with a light on top of it?" Another miner saw it this way: "Coal or not, we're striking." Old R.J. James, a fish coal miner who had put sixty years of his life into the mine told me, "I was born a fish coal miner and I'll die a fish coal miner." And he did die later that day, but not before singing the terrific coal miner's song, the lyrics of which cannot be printed here due to copyright restrictions.

HOW RECYCLING WORKS IN UTAH

STOMACHS OF THE SEA

There is debate about how many stomachs there are in the sea. Experts say 400, while some other people say 450 or more. The sea is dark. The water marlin has six stomachs, all in a row like a necklace. Jellyfish are mostly stomach. The stomach of the sea manatee is unique in that it is large enough to hold a conveyor. Some historians talk about how interesting it is that barracudas speak Spanish. And some speak Catalán. This is not of interest. Nor is it interesting that many barracudas are named Ignacio and want to direct films. You will reap what you sow. This is the essential lesson of the Bible and other stories in books. And keep your papers in boxes. Keep your framed pictures in boxes. Keep all of your possessions in boxes, and stack these boxes neatly in rows. Put these rows in the garage and show the boxes to guests on holidays. When your guests leave, shake their hands and look into their eyes. Tell them the truth about their lives and wave goodbye. The boxes should be labeled on the top and on three sides in clear capital letters. When the flood comes, the boxes will be carried out to sea to be eaten by the stomachs in the ocean. Barracudas also know some German.

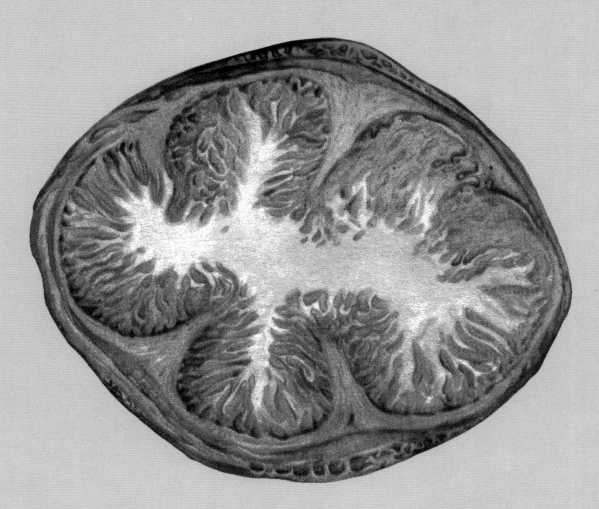

WHEN YOU ARE BEING EATEN BY A MANATEE, THIS PICTURE ABOVE WILL BE THE
LAST THING YOU WILL SEE. WHEN YOU SEE IT NEXT, AS YOUR TORSO IS RIPPED FROM
YOUR LEGS, THE THRASHING WILL MAKE IT DIFFICULT TO SEE. STUDY THE IMAGE NOW.

MATCH THE ANIMALS OF THE OCEAN TO THE KIND OF FOOD THEY EAT

ANIMALS	FOOD
1. BARRACUDA	A. CARROTS
2. SHARK	B. INK [A JAR OF BLACK INK]
3. WHALE	C. CHILDREN
4. GIANT SQUID	D. FRUIT ROLLS
5. ANGELFISH	E. GRANDMOTHERS
6. TURTLE	F. MOUNTAIN DEW AND SNACKWELL'S CREAM-FILLED COOKIES
7. DOLPHIN	G. WHITE PEOPLE DRESSED AS NATIVE AMERICANS

ANSWERS: 1. G AND C, 2. C, 3. E AND C, 4. F AND C, 5. A AND C, 6. B AND C, 7. D AND C

FIND THE FAKES

Camouflage is a key mechanism of defense and survival and attractiveness in the deep ocean—not as important as a flattened molars or leg fat, maybe, but still, it possesses a certain significance. Some sea dwellers have learned to alter the color of their skin to look like something inedible, like a chimichanga with ranch dressing; some have learned to paint their stomach to look like the face of a whistling man. A few have gotten so good at disguising themselves that they can be next to impossible to detect. But with some experience, and insight, and a great deal of sleep, the imposters can be unmasked. Pictured here are seven fakes mingling in a crowed of (approximately) fifty-seven reals. Can you spot the pretenders?

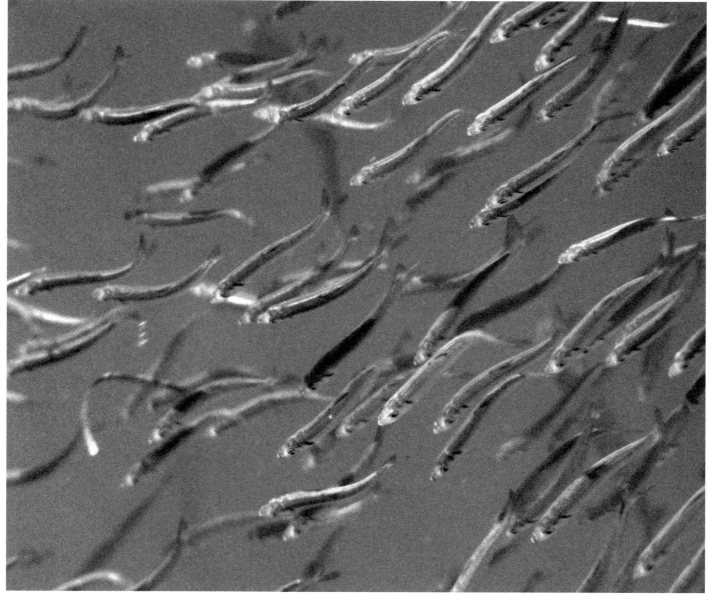

SARDINE, SARDINE, GROUPER, SARDINE, SARDINE
SQUID, SARDINE, SARDINE, SARDINE, SARDINE, SARDINE, SARDINE, SARDINE, SQUID, SARDINE, SARDINE,
SARDINE, SARDINE, SARDINE, SARDINE, SARDINE, SQUID, SARDINE, SARDINE, SARDINE, SARDINE, SARDINE,
SQUID, SARDINE, SARDINE, SARDINE, SARDINE, SARDINE, SARDINE, SARDINE, SARDINE, SQUID, SARDINE, SARDINE,
ANSWER (IN COUNTER-CLOCKWISE ORDER, STARTING WITH THE TOTALLY FAKE ONE IN THE UPPER-LEFT):

53
AoTo

WHAT KINDS OF MUSIC DO GIANT SQUIDS LISTEN TO WHILE TRAVELING BY TRAIN?

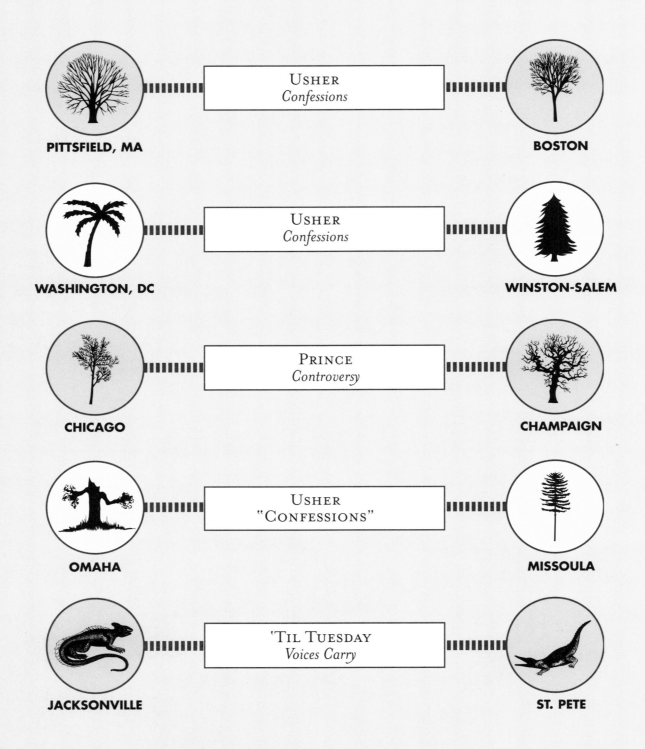

PITTSFIELD, MA — USHER *Confessions* — **BOSTON**

WASHINGTON, DC — USHER *Confessions* — **WINSTON-SALEM**

CHICAGO — PRINCE *Controversy* — **CHAMPAIGN**

OMAHA — USHER "Confessions" — **MISSOULA**

JACKSONVILLE — 'TIL TUESDAY *Voices Carry* — **ST. PETE**

Note: Music first came to the ocean by way of merchant marines in the late nineteenth century and also the Sixties during the time of that one woman. When the animals of the ocean first encountered music, they thought it sounded faint. And sometimes muffled. Some rye bread is Jewish and some is Russian. In the movie called *Tron*, there are men and women in tight clothing who throw discs and drive cars. Their world is not so different than ours. Bless us all.

CAN YOU IDENTIFY WHICH OF THESE TRAINS ARE FAMOUS, AND WHICH ARE USELESS?

THE ADVENTURE OF GUNTHER, THE LANTERNFISH WHO WANTED TO SCOPE OUT THIS ONE PART OF THIS COOL CORAL REEF REAL QUICK

This is the story of Gunther, the lanternfish, who was not liked by anyone. Because he was not liked, Gunther left his native fish village and traveled East. This is the first story ever written about a lanternfish because lanternfish are liars. They deceive people and are all eventually eaten by porpoises, as was Gunther. He was talking about clip art one day, making nasty jokes about clip art, when he was eaten whole by a porpoise. Sea otters hang out by these deposit areas because they are tough. Scientists estimate only two otters are needed to kill a full-grown human. But we are also getting bigger as a people, probably thanks to all the high bars there are to hang from. The Mayans were small people but they could still believe in things like bloodletting and snakes. Mel Gibson believes in the Mayans and he is making a movie about them but for him it is no biggie. A lot happens in spring. Not just in terms of sales but also in nature. Plants grow and change color but you rarely hear about that in the news. People often say read between the lines but sometimes that's not always realistic. I figure if you make a penny every day and keep a penny every day then that's a great start. After that it's a lot about viral marketing. But Gunther was not eaten. He is prospering. In fact Gunther is a wealthy adventure capitalist in Finance City! He is doing very well and has all the things he could ever want in life, such as flavored gum, and he has almost no need for a headstone or a memorial plaque because he is quite alive. So alive is he that he often jokes with his friends about being alive and how nice that is with his friends who were also laughing at being 100 percent alive and none of whom were festering in the entrails of a porpoise because of their wicked lanternfish lies.

DID YOU KNOW?

THE WORLD'S MOST VALUABLE PAIR OF KHAKIS IS LOCATED IN MOROCCO. THEY ARE GUARDED BY THIS MAN PICTURED AT LEFT. THIS MAN WEARING THESE CLOTHES. THE KHAKIS CAN BE VISITED YEAR-ROUND.

THE MAN ABOVE WHO GUARDS THE KHAKIS HAS A GOOD HOME LIFE. STABLE AND ENJOYABLE. HE LIKES TO ACT; HE PUTS ON PLAYS WITH HIS CHILDREN AND NEIGHBORS.

THESE PLAYS ARE TRAGEDIES, PRIMARILY. VERY DRAMATIC. HE SOMETIMES WATCHES THE BUTCHERS ON THEIR WAY TO MARKET IN THE MORNINGS, AND HE BREATHES IN THE DESERT AIR. AND WHEN HE DOES THIS, HE WONDERS ABOUT THE CLOTHES HE IS REQUIRED TO WEAR WHILE GUARDING THE KHAKIS. HE THINKS THE SHIRT IS TOO BLOUSY, AND THE SHOES HAVE RED BALLS AT THE END. WHEN HE WAS GROWING UP, HE DID NOT IMAGINE HE WOULD BE WEARING SUCH AN OUTFIT AND GUARDING VALUABLE PANTS. AND WHEN HE GOT THIS JOB, HE WAS UNSURE HOW LONG HE WOULD KEEP IT. BUT HE HAS KEPT THE JOB FOR FOURTEEN YEARS, AND HIS THREE CHILDREN WERE RAISED WITH THE PROCEEDS FROM THIS JOB. JUST A WEEK AGO HE PUT ON A PRODUCTION OF *Three Days of Rain*, AND HE THOUGHT HIS CHILDREN PERFORMED WELL. HIS NEIGHBORS WERE NOT GOOD, THOUGH, AND HE WILL NOT CAST THEM AGAIN.

WHY MOST GIANT SQUIDS WILL NOT WATCH TV IN BLACK AND WHITE

I have interviewed hundreds of giant squids for this book, and without exception—with only a dozen or so exceptions—they refuse to watch TV shows broadcast in black and white. I asked them why, even though I knew the answer.

One of the squids I interviewed was very nervous during the interview, and was wearing stained clothing that was also knitted. I did not trust this interview subject and asked him to leave my office. He became belligerent and knocked over a chair. He was really unappealing in every way, and I fear there are too many more out there just like him. Sometimes I think squids are a stupid animal to be studying.

Growing up, I never thought I would be spending so much time researching cuttlefish. I sometimes think I went wrong somewhere. I blame Benny for much of this. The squid thing was his idea. But he's in the garden right now, putting dirt into jars, so I can't yell at him. After he puts the dirt in jars, he stacks them in the basement.

ANIMALS OF THE OCEAN THAT ARE NOT WORTH DISCUSSING

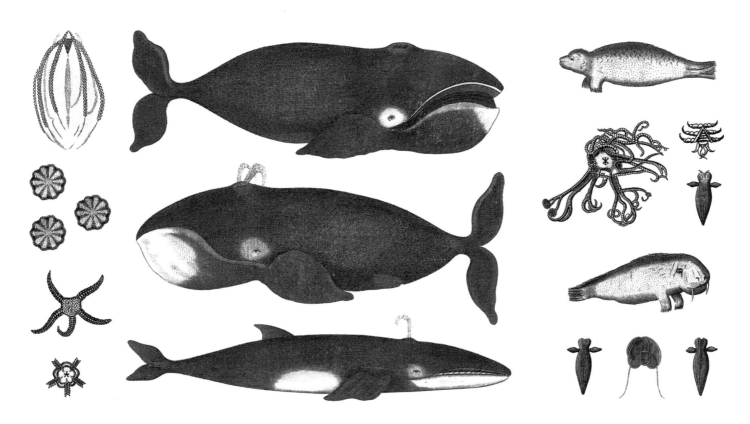

THE RULES OF ENGAGEMENT

Each year in February, giant bull squid congregate in cold waters to engage in a ritual designed to determine the pecking order the following year.

With fierce bellows, seven cards are dealt to each male squid, all except for the dealer, who gets eight cards. One card is placed face UP in the middle, and the rest of the cards are placed face DOWN next to the one card that was placed facing UP. The first male squid to play, the male squid sitting two seats to the right of the dealer, must match the card facing UP. For example, if the card is a Seven of Hearts, the male squid must throw down a Seven of Spades, or a Seven of Diamonds, or a Seven of Clubs, or a Three of Hearts along with a Four of Spades or an Ace of Diamonds and a Six of Hearts or a Three of Spades and a Two of Diamonds and a Two of Clubs. If ever a male squid finds himself without a matching card or cards, he must pick a card from the DRAW pile until he gets a card that does match. In special situations, for example the male squid to the LEFT of the dealer refuses to go get more chips even though he is sitting closest to the kitchen, the dealer may play a Wild Draw Sixteen card.

When a male squid has reduced his hand to just one card, he hums a tune of his own devising and blushes deeply. This causes the other bull squids to drop their cards in confusion. If the other male squids do not drop their cards in confusion, the blushing squid must draw two cards. The last and only male squid left holding one card is declared the winner, and the winner is permitted to carry small pillows (otherwise forbidden).

THE MEANING OF SQUID BLUSHING

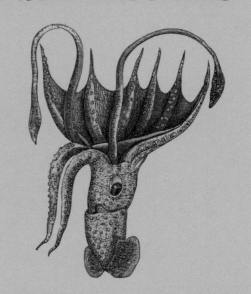

MISINTERPRETING A GIANT SQUID'S BLUSHING CAN BE NOT ONLY SHAMING, IT CAN BE DEADLY. IT IS NOT VERY COMPLICATED, THOUGH. WHEN A SQUID BLUSHES BURGUNDY, IT MEANS HE IS THIRSTY AND SHOULD BE GIVEN WATER. WHEN A SQUID BLUSHES ANY OTHER COLOR, ITS MEANING IS DEADLY. THE DEATH WILL COME QUICKLY, AND IT WILL NOT BE KNOWN WHO THE VICTIM IS UNTIL THAT VICTIM IS DEAD. ONE OF THE GREAT FILMS OF THE LAST FORTY YEARS IS *Tron*.

IS IT DEDUCTIBLE?

Proper preparation for deep-sea research requires a great deal of equipment, which can cost hundreds of thousands of money. Happily, due to government ignorance and the treachery of accountants worldwide, most of this equipment can be written off at tax time. The important thing is knowing which things are deductible and which things are only deductible if you call them something else on the forms. I have had three separate sets of cousins who together made a flag of Peru out of plywood and dried fruit. And those plastic bread-baggie clips, what are they called? You should save those. I have convinced many nautical people that these clips are a form of underwater currency.

DEDUCTIBLE

Air tanks
Air that goes in tanks

Snacks
Printer cartridges
Goggles
Flippers
Submersible pod
Food
Food for dinner

Gas to get to the ocean
Nightsticks
Hair plugs
Glare screens
Wire Cutters
Tar mats
Alabaster countertop

Trowels
Loupes (both types)

Magnetic Arms
Babies (having)

Sombreros
Electric Razors
Crutches
Steel-toed boots
Calipers (medicinal)
Ergonomic footrest
Other footrest
Massages

NOT DEDUCTIBLE

Wicker furniture for submersible pod
Sunscreen
Robes
Bejeweled throne

Extra set of keys
Plastic ficus
Chalk Art

Subscription to newsmagazine
Autographed baseballs and bats

Flowers for Secretary's Day
Babies (owning)
Bolo tie
Straws
Straw

THE MID-ATLANTIC GREY SHARK'S GUIDE TO INSTALLING FLOOR TILE

PROJECT:
Floor Tile Installation
(for Mid-Atlantic Grey Sharks)

SKILL LEVEL:
2-3 (Basic to Moderate)

TIME TAKEN:
2 Hours

TOOLS REQUIRED:
- **Tiles**
- **Primer**
- **Durock**
- **Trowel**
- **Cement-board screws**
- **Fiberglass mesh tape**

PROJECT NOTES:
If you are a shark and are doing a large room with only one entrance, you will start laying tile at the back of the room and work outward.

Sometimes the only practical approach is to lay tiles on one half of the room during the first day, so you can walk on them the next day when finishing the job.

Many times in life, grey sharks need to install floor tile, but it is very difficult for most of them to do so. It is best to start with the installation of tile in a small space, for example a closet. This is easy enough for a carnivorous animal in the Mid-Atlantic. Here is a guide to installing floor tile if you are a shark in the ocean.

First, purchase some plain beige 6" x 6" tiles. They will cost 25 cents each, or $1 a square foot. Most sharks are on a budget, and this is much cheaper than the marble tiles, which can cost up to $6 per square foot.

Second, vacuum the floor and paint it with oil-based primer. Next, you will need a tile-backer board. Cut out a piece of 1/2" Durock to fit in the closet, and test the fit before mixing any mortar. Apply a layer of thin set mortar to the floor, using the smooth edge of the trowel to force the mud into the cracks in the floorboards.

Using the notched side of the trowel (1/4" x 1/4" square notches) now comb the mortar into a series of ridges. Now lay the Durock into place. The 1/2" Durock in place, step on the cement board to press it into the mortar.

Now drive in Rock-On™ brand of cement-board screws. Some sharks use roofing nails to install cement-board. If you do, be sure to hit the floor joists. If you stick with screws, which is the only non-stupid way to do it, place the screws about 8" apart.

At the seam, apply a strip of fiberglass mesh tape. This will be covered with mortar as soon as you begin to lay tiles.

Laying out a straight reference line for the tiles is crucial, especially in large rooms. Use a 12" speed-square to obtain a right angle, and align a chalk line with the edge.

Tile Time:

Spread some thin set mortar on the Durock, and be careful not to obscure the chalk line. Use the smooth edge to squeeze the mortar into the rough surface.

Now use the notched side to comb out the mortar. The ridges are necessary to afford the ability to push the tile down into the mortar. Otherwise the mortar will ooze out around the edges.

Lay a couple of tiles against the spacers, and add more spacers as you progress. These spacers act as a reliable guide, keeping the gap uniform and keeping the tiles aligned.

Soon you will be finished.

A GUIDE TO INSTALLING DECORATIVE ENTRYWAY TILE

IN CLOSING

I am as exhausted as you are. Now listen before you rest and I rest and Benny puts his shirt back on. Do not waste your time thinking of birds or topiary. Most postage stamps are fraudulent and I can prove it. Most miners have never been underground and they know it. All of the people of Norway are in fact Dutch. Do not borrow money from anyone from the South, or anyone who has been to the South. Do not go to Ohio. Do not speak to Dutch people pretending to be Norwegians from Ohio. Read now and future HOW books and then burn them. Wail uncontrollably when you burn them. Go see your neighbors and deceive them. When they ask for help with their roofing do not believe them. It is war when you speak to the people with eyes such as theirs. People have worn orange shirts in every major decade and this is important only in how it relates to the fact that I have loved you all from the start. No one will take away this feeling.

. . . .

UPCOMING TITLES IN THE H-O-W SERIES

Metal and Metal Storage

Hanging Heavy Things on Walls

Cold Fusion

Surgery

Quicksand

Glass in the Wild

Mortar

Gas and Gas Usage

How to Eat

Talking to Babies Underwater

Planet Removal

Tall Men

Using Bottles to Cause Injury

Yellowcake: Sales and Marketing in Central Africa

Music and Mountain Installation

Flower Construction

Magazine Reading

Sharpness

Mind Control

Airline Clothing

You, Me, and the National Society of Allotment and Leisure Gardeners (NSALG) Makes Three

ABOUT THE AUTHORS

Dr. Doris Haggis-On-Whey now has eighteen degrees from twenty institutions of higher learning and carpentry. She has traveled the world extensively, so much in fact that there are those who believe that Dr. H-O-W actually invented the world. This is not in fact true. But she has written or will soon write over 156 definitive and Earth-changing books on such subjects as Advanced Electricity Usage, Puppetry, Cooking Food without Using Food, Orange Paper, Thrones, Orangeish-Yellow Paper, Post Office Design and Operation, Calculus for People from Small Towns, and Grease Theory and Construction.

Benny is the husband of Dr. Doris Haggis-On-Whey, and is hiding in the van.

ABOUT THE DESIGNERS

Mark Wasserman and Irene Ng continue to have the privilege of working with Dr. Haggis-On-Whey. As they have chosen to not pursue a life of science, they are hardly worth discussing here.

Research assistance has been provided by the de la Manzana brothers, and by Dave and Toph Eggers.